MW00625362

20/20 DIVISION

20/20 DIVISION

Wallace Johnson

To Rebecca

Continue to love and the light will be there.

Wallace Jol

20/20 DIVISION copyright © 2020 by Wallace Johnson. All rights reserved. Printed by 48 Hour Books. No part of this book may be used or reproduced in any manner whatsoever without written permission of the copyright owner.

Book design by C J Johnson

www.wallacejohnsonauthor.com

Library of Congress Number: 8977391878

Dedicated
to all the innocent lives lost
in the struggle

Contents

Acknowledgments

To my peeps – I appreciate and cherish all of you. Thanks to God for creating the universe that continually provides inspiration. Thank you to Mom and Dad for creating the foundation. Special thanks to Cyndi, Tyson, Dallion, and Kingston for constantly providing the motivation.

Preface

Inspired by God and the happenings leading up to and including the year 2020, this book contains thoughts and feelings pertaining to many life events experienced by humanity and told through the perspectives of various points of view. It will hopefully open some eyes and provide insight into how different we aren't and similar we are. We ultimately have the same wants and needs, but are shaped by different journeys.

Introduction

A natural born lyricist, Wallace Johnson melds his adoration for rap lyrics with powerful poetic wordplay. In 20/20 DIVISION, his soul absorbs the pain of the oppressed until it floods through his bars, breaking all boundaries and shining truth into the places less thought of and thought less of. Read, listen, and see.

~C J Johnson

Chapter 1: 20/20 Vision

"We need unity

not

qualified immunity"

Wallace Johnson

20/20 Vision

I see unblinded misery
unmasked tragedy

I view the misconstrued
exposing their detest of dark hues

I peer at my peers
queer and peculiar
with chants and cheers

I squint at the obsession with tints
I open my eyes to the likes and replies
The facades and lies

I see clearly the high definition
of societal deep-rooted incisions

I see the stars
for the lack of cars

Polluting the air with shootings
and lootings

Masked, but yet I gaze
Amazed at the last days

The Devil

The Devil is running for president
and the so-called Christians are voting

The Devil is campaigning
and media keeps requoting

The Devil is running for president
and leading in the polls

Satan is getting support . . . say it ain't so

His campaign pitch delivered
with silver forked tongue

Spewing hatred and negatively . . . run, run, run

The Devil is running
and followers are steady chasing

Satan is winning
and the racers hearts are racing

Viral Gone

Protests, Pandemic, Police
People, Power, Peace

Peaceful protests
Civil unrest
Pitiful president with puffed out chest

Photo ops
posts Photoshopped
police brutality, crooked cops

Panic, Pandemic, Paradox - systemic
Pressure to the pulse
of your own people

presidential
political stunt posing with Psalms
in palm

Inflicting more harm
Suppressing the calm

Protests, Pandemic, Prisons - Systemic
Racist police
No justice, No peace

Awakening

There's no mistaking
The great awakening
Flags and buildings burning
Distance learning
Stomachs turning
Guts wrenching
Suicidal hangings, lynchings
Face coverings
Statues toppling after hovering
Mass testing
Civil unresting
presidential downward spiral
Covid-19 gone viral
Police, brutal
Reform attempts, futile
Shelves barren
Screaming Karens
Crying president
Dying residents
Lying president
Crying residents

Convenient Submissiveness

president divisive
Keep the indentured submissive
Kneeling at they feet
Whitewash and repeat
The cycle never ending
Generations never mending
Not even pretending
The message that they sending
At least humor me with
a false rumor D
about future reparations
and about how you plan to unite the nation
Keep the cycle going
'til it's pearly white and snowing
Keep them on their knees and praying
while you feign Christian obeyance
while you say be grateful
while your hearts stay hateful
Keep them on their knees
at Lincoln's feet
Keep them on their knees
in the plantation heat
But when that sweet song plays
Get on your feet!

The Youth

The youth are the truth
Hit 'em hard at the booths
Deface them
Replace them -
statuesque standing
Reform demanding
Losses we handing
Good ole networks disbanding
The youth are the truth
Hit 'em at the booths

False Idols

False idols
of confederation
toppling over the foundation
of a nation
beheading the serpents
of a slithery equation
representing the brutality and molestation
smothering equality
Where's the reparations?
Articles of confederation
particles of separation
Feel like We under sedation
Where's our reparations?

Suffocating

People unemployed
Planned pandemic
War against racism, systemic

God's plan, 2020 Vision
exposing the wounds of racism
with precise incisions

Leader's jaded insight, inciting riots,
hoarding, feeding steady diets
of greed and ignoring those in need

From Birthday parades
to parades of protestors

Funeral processions
for Breonna, Ahmaud and Floyd

Brutal cops, burning businesses,
buildings destroyed

Military deployed
Loss of freedoms once enjoyed

It's SUFFOCATING

Defense

Immense
police defense
shield the president
as he threatens residents

Protest the protests with disgust
Protect the statues and busts
of confederate losers
human abusers

It's a riot how they
denounce riots
attack the character of Blacks
lash out at looters
racist comments as they sit at their computers
Praise peaceful, quiet demonstrations
as they scream "All lives matter" in this
hypocritical nation

Behind The Shield

The power I wield
behind the shield
plants seeds in the killing fields
The power never yields
Scars unhealed
plants seeds in the killing fields
The seeds I sow
I reap and grow
off Black backs, tears, blood and tracks
The fate is sealed
wounds unhealed
through the power of the shield
I will never yield
my supreme birthrights,
never yield to the plight
of the oppressed -
so obsessed with justness
I savor in the fruits of the shield
I yield
Nothing
I bask in the light
that the darkness provides
Behind the great shield I hide

Discovery

They say
that I have any easier way,
but I work hard, just like any other man
How is it that I have a so-called upper hand?

Is it because . . .
I'm profiled at a lesser rate?
Have a lower death rate?
Seen as non-threatening in a job interview?
Not badgered by the boys in blue?
When sleeping in my lounge dorm,
not presumed to be out of decorum?
When on my own property, jiggling my keys,
not assumed to be committing thievery?
My child, clenching chips or a toy gun
is not mistaken for having a real weapon?
I turn on the TV and constantly see
people that represent me positively?
In a store I see more and more
products suited for
my complexion in every section?
Fortunately, disproportionately, and historically
we are the majority
We are business leaders, media moguls and
lawmakers,
the merciless rights takers
I inherited a pearly path with less obstacles,

a bright white network that is so optimal
I enjoy the absence of suspicion
and the ability to act on my own volition
I move about, consume, work and freely play
Maybe the privilege does exist, to my dismay.

Fallen

Tillman's a hero
but Kap is zero?
Martyrdom over
Stardom
Stand for something
Fall for nothing
Kneel to propose
and oppose
Fall for the love
Felled for love

Stand Pat

His life came to an end
at the hands of a friend
It's hard to comprehend
But let's not pretend
The army maintained
he was ambushed on terrain
He gave up the glory
deserved a better ending story
He stood

Unity

We need unity
Not qualified immunity
Understanding
Less reprimanding
Community policing
Stop the looting and fleecing
Repair the cogs
With open dialogue
Sit down with a beverage
Exercise our leverage
Speak the truth unmasked
Take each other to task

What Matters

Blue lives
Black lives
Piercing knives
One cuts deeper
severing arteries
of generational qualities
White lives, Black lives
It's a matter
of blood splatter
How much blood spilled?
How many more killed
on God's green Earth
on God's Brown turf?
What's a life worth
right from the birth?

Chapter 2:
First Sight

"My skin

is

my sin"

Wallace Johnson

Entrance

Following repeated movements
thrusts and pushes
I have emerged
I have made a gallant entrance
        Here I am, I say
if that vernacular was possible

Not what I expected
startled, I cry upon entrance
Bright, hostile environment
I recollect warmth and timely nourishment
Is it possible to resubmerge?
Somehow, I still feel connected to the warmth

Sharp, shiny, blunt approaching
I feel freedom and attachment
unexplainable
A world of giants
What is my role?
Where is my place?

Dry Fish

I'm a nigger in the suburbs
that's how I'm viewed
Either way you look at it, I'm screwed
Whites don't want me in their neighborhood
They think I will be up to no good
Blacks think I'm too good to hang in the hood

Surrounded by Whites every day, *I* can cope
It is some of *them* who want me hangin by a rope
Some call me "buddy" to my face
but behind my back they insult my race
They can't fool me! I can see it in their eyes
My skin color, they despise
You should've seen their expressions
when we moved in
Some looked like we committed
a grave sin

They hope the habitation won't increase -
that their lily white neighborhood
will remain in peace
They consider a "good hood" mainly White
When other races move in, they are in fright
They're afraid because
all they know is what they've seen on TV
I'm just a nigger in the suburbs -
that's how they see me.

Slur

Don't say it
Don't you dare
It's offensive, I swear
It hurts
Don't blurt it
It cuts so deep,
censored with a bleep
Don't utter
It's like knives thru butter
Don't say it

Tire Tracks

I awoke at dawn -
tire tracks on my lawn
Was it because they couldn't stand to see
a rich green lawn landscaped so nicely?

On another day a few weeks back
I again awoke to deep tire tracks
I began to think: *Is it because we're Black?*

What would possess someone to repeat this
senseless act
again and again
over a significant span
on our land?

We awoke to deep tire treads
I wondered is it something we did or said?
Over and over - repeat, repeat
Was it due to being the only Black family
on the street?

It wasn't only our terrain you scarred
When we try to gain an inch
you wanna take our yard.

Robbers and Robbers

Let's play "Robbers and Robbers"
portraying those who robbed us
of our dignity and youth
those that stole and hid the truth
those that refused to use discretion
those so quick to draw their weapons

Let's play "Police the Police"
for those that robbed and fleeced
the unarmed lives
stole husbands from wives
took sons from mothers
those that choked and smothered
theft of the breaths
Till no heartbeats were left

Let's play authority figure
Do our part to exterminate niggers
Let's flex our blue power
with the use of gun powder
and mighty choke holds
Till the Black bodies go cold.

Let's play "Robbers and Robbers"
Till Black dignity is clobbered
Let's refuse to relinquish our stranglehold

Truth be told,
we have a full house
which we will never fold

Let's blast them in the back as they scurry away
Let's use real guns and kill them in the Park
in the light of day
> *I couldn't see. It was dark,* we'll say
> *I feared for my life.*
> *He was a very large schoolboy.*
12 years old, toting a toy

Let's kneel with joy
Aim and destroy
Clever and coy
Shame and destroy

So let's play "Robbers and Robbers"
and keep America great
preserve the values of these Divided
States of Hate.

Second Date

There will be no second date
with some second rate
Citizen
There will be hell to pay, you'll be disciplined

I'm perplexed - thought we had a good time
You said you liked me and that I was "sooo fine"
It blows my mind. I can't comprehend
Were your feelings for me just pretend?
You fawned over me
Now we can only be . . . friends?
You said you really enjoyed my company
You even mentioned I was husbandly
So why suddenly the 180 degree?

Oh I see, it must be me
Now I get why your daddy was staring,
glaring so heavily
He forbade and forebode,
hollered and crowed
Contested with detest so irately
There will be no second date with the likes of me.

They didn't take time to see,
view my impressive pedigree
or that I was destined for a Master's degree
They didn't care to inquire
about my inner desires -

an athlete, a writer, a gentleman
they failed to discover due to their endeavors
to prevent us from becoming lovers
They detested, protested, so intently
There will be no second date with the likes of me.

Sign Here

Please sign this autograph
but not these marriage papers
You're safe, but
the rest of you are rapers
Entertain us all
bouncing that ball
Just don't think
your dating or mating
You sign this autograph -
just can't sign
these papers

little white lives

Have you ever been white-balled?
Or called
the white sheep of the family?
Or lost all your money on white Monday or
Tuesday?
Or have you been threatened with
a white mark on your record?
Have you ever been suspected
of being a sunny character
or using shiny humor?
It's so tragic
that you've never been accused of
using white magic
Have you ever been a light horse in a race?
So sad
Has your race ever been associated with . . .
being bad?

Falling Sky

The sky is falling
or am I upside down?
The globe is spinning
or am I going round?
Don't come around here thinking you the man
Better have some alternate plan
Gonna reign on our parade?
You might feel the wrath of the blades
We run shit in this domain
Bullets to your brain
This turf is in our possession
Playin with lethal weapons
Control is the game
Makin a name
for yourself
Who you representin?
I'm ventin
anger 'cause we can't get out the blocks
Got us sellin rocks
Seems the only way, I can get by
College? Why try
Curriculum's weak
Fluently, can't speak
I'm better off livin the trife life
Got kids, but no wife
Some say I'm deadbeat
Gotta always pack heat
Keep my stash neat

Gotta supply my kids with heat
Everything equal, don't make me laugh
I'm livin in a blood bath
While the president's go no worries
I'm watchin roaches scurry
Barrel of crabs
pull me back in
My skin is my sin
We can't win
Keep strivin

Playground Legend

I hate to be the bearer of bad news
but your boy has been killed by a rival crew
Now pallbearers will lift him
We will cremate and sift him
spread his ashes over the playground
That is where he could always be found
on weekends wit his friends
He had the "butter" jump shot
Now he got shot
He ran around the city
doin extracurricular activities
Flippin ki's
This dog had fleas
I'll think of him when the wind blows
When I smoke endo
tappin my joint ashes out my window

Welling

My eyelids overflow
welling with wellness
spelling my helplessness
flooding my sadness

My eyes well with the sorrow
wish well for tomorrow
flow with the streams
nightmares and dreams
deliver the rivers of aspiration
the precipitation of belief
the hopes, anticipation

My eyes well with compassion
empathy I fashion
My eyes spill
for the blood, the kill
the strength, the will
the rights, the bills

My eyes spew
for the many, the few
the darkness hue
my heart heavy with rue
my eyes gaze
through the fogginess of haze
the pupils of craze

My eyes pour for the poor
the misguided and weak
the battered and meek
It flows down my cheek
for those that misspeak
or mistakenly misspoke

My eyes stay woke

Chapter 3:
Hind Sight

"distorting the stories

snatching the glory"

Not You

This current situation
is a staunch reminder
of who is really in control

Unfair Skin

My skin is my gift
but I didn't ask for it
The superiority of my pigment
is just a figment
of your imagination,
a pitiful culmination of your frustration

They say my skin is a privilege from birth
and I'm entitled to more on this Earth
Presently my pure presence
is considered a present
my lightness, my whiteness
my pallidity, my brightness
My skin so pristine and fair
How dare they suggest it provides an edge-
That's so unfair

Race

One day we'll fulfill
the promise of a checkered past
slowly though
no checkered flag
Patriots say no colored rag
can be disrespected by no colored fag

We will inform you when it's time
to form a picket line
when it's right to fight the lengthy fight
conveniently die for your rights

We'll provide permits and signs
inform you when it's fine
for you to Rage Against the Machine
or Fight the Power
only acceptable at this exact hour

It's got to feel comfortable and peaceful
as you tread ever so lightly
As you march and rant,
do so delicately
As you chant with a whisper
soft as a whisker
No not that way. This way - approved
No needle moved
Preserve the status
feed the status quo

Pay

You gon pay
if you don't pay attention
I'm not in your immediate mentions
It's causing dissension

Feces

You say I am a lower species
Why you talkin feces?
I am original man.
That means I am pre-
while you are post
Before
After
but you got the laughter
'cause you know we are buried deep like treasure
Ahh clever
Remember Evers?
And Tuskegee?
But I am pre-
Are we?
Yes.
Then why are we behind and not in front?
Comin up short like bunts
My brain is waterlogged
That's why
young men die, babies cry
while the opposition sighs
Can we rise up from the ashes?
and infiltrate the masses?
The elements -
solid, liquid, and gaseous
Get your foot off me so I can stand
in back, but
Original Man.

Property

You got me -
property
of yours
so much that I ooze through your pores
attached at the hip, almost joined
my baby, the phrase coined
You're mine - we even have certification
Oh! What a nation
Can't possess another, just one
that's how we keep trust in someone
Fidelity or slavery?
Look what I've done for you!
Look what you gave to me
If we part, I'm entitled
the house and the car title
for the pain inflicted
I'm a victim

The Slaveflower

As a result of glocks and rocks
keys go into locks
held by founders of Plymouth Rock
Crack! That does break Mama's back -
and spirits. Causing her to whine, fine
designer clothes, the steel doors and bars
entrapping candy coated, caramel choc-o-late
treated like shit
Exhibit
heart palpitations caused by a systematic nation
based on equations:
Caucasians + invasions = abrasions
Band together to aid each brother
sister we soothe blisters
from Mr. Massa-chu-shits
but don't swallow it
There will be justice well served
well deserved -
what they got. Shot
of whiskey. It was risky
behavior. But got away Francis Scott Free
the slaves. Abe Lincoln wasn't thinkin about Black
America the beautifull of shit - happens
to be my Mother - land
Africa - go back! They laugh at ya
They brought us here
is where I live
Free or die.

Trails of Tears

Trails of tears
Blood Stains from fears
Clogged up ears
for years
refusing to hear
the ugly cheers, the boos and jeers
Covering up the scars of what got us here
Cosmetically, aesthetically
band-aiding the raiding
pillaging and plundering the
surgical masking of the blundering
After the killing and taming
after the slaughtering and maiming,
honors with naming
lakes and territories
then distorting the stories
snatching the glory
It implores me
to expose
those that chose
to oppress and impose
those that pilfered and pillaged
and scorched the villages
those that lie to the pupils in text
The scoundrels that leave us vexed

Crow's feet

Crows land on your eyes
right at the corners
Worn out, everyday laborer
Pinch my nerves, wake me
from this nightmare
Ridin my back, breakin
Folk worked their asses
now missin
walkin 'round
assless, less pride
less monetary figure
it out for me
I can't
Yes, you can.
Men of war, battling for what?
For who?
Freedom? Shit! that's
freely dumb

Subjugation

Subjugation
Methods of a nation
Birth rights guarded
Resistance bombarded
Battered and tattered
Torn and worn
Battles for chattel
Ruptured and rattled
Sold like cattle
Front lines of the battles
Syphilis civil-less
Civil war, civil unrest
Supreme quest
Supreme being
Believing is seeing
Forever disagreeing
Forever opposed
Souls disposed
He arose,
ascended, arose

Black Wall Street

I had kept my property so neat
on Black Wall Street
I swept my steps with pride and esteem
on Black Wall Street
I stepped with confidence in my feet
as I flourished and danced down
Black Wall Street
I felt very alive
My people prospered and thrived
on Black Wall Street
We minded our businesses,
kept safe distances
on Black Wall Street
We had something to call ours
until the Devils and cowards descended
on Black Wall Street
Then came the looting and shooting
the hollering and hooting
the burning and torching
the lynchings and scorching
on Black Wall Street
The bloodshed of the dead
the streets flooded with red
My people were murdered in numbers
akin to Red Summer
on Black Wall Street

History & Herstory

All of the History and Herstory
buried in the cemetery
All of the souls
of the decomposed
Don't you care or wonder
if they still hear the thunder?
Or if they still marvel at the moonlight
on a Friday night?
They are forgotten
as they lie rotting
Only flesh eating parasites pay any mind
to the remains of mankind
Shouldn't we pay attention?
Maybe he died from a lynching
or maybe she fought with friends
without ability to make amends
You have to believe only the skeletons remain,
what moves on are the contents of the brain
the memories and the spirits
the souls and their lyrics
Too often we disrespect the grave
Lovers use it to misbehave
We are taught to be scared
As you ride by with tunes blared
Some even desecrate -
these cowardice crimes of hate
Don't you know that this is where you will go
when you meet your fate?

Here

How did we get here?
where the fear
outweighs the common sense
and the leveled become dense?
The children are painted with a
brush of hatred
and the artist created it
with a palate of evil
Vile human beings
got us here
A place so barren
where savages are raring
to go . . . here

Chapter 4: Introspection

"repair the damage

of living -

Liver Damage"

Touched

Where does inspiration come from?
Is it the hand of God touching upon thee?
Is it that that is within me
surfacing at opportune moments
once suppressed by outside forces?
Suddenly exposed like worms in rainfall?
I sometimes don't recall
what the dreams produce

Does it come from being under the gun?
Wish I recorded the inspiration
Sudden sensation caressing my brain
into spectacular thoughts
Supplying my mind with classic verses
not rehearsed,
written down before dispersed
It's a curse for the ages
Sages sprinkled on pages
Outrageous, Courageous
Contagious

Ruptured Spirit

Ruptured spirit
Distorted soul
Convoluted refuted
Polluted executed
for the exact actions
of various factions
Exacerbated interactions
can't gain, attain any traction
Momentum slowed
Snail's pace
Turtle's race
Slow and steady
Tactical and heady
Stay ready, chambered
Oppose being endangered
Motivated and angered
Inspired and wired
Driven and ambitious
Invigorated and viscous
Treacherous and reckless
Spotless and speckless
Clean squeaky
Forked tongue and cheeky
Inheritors - the meekly
Assenting weekly
Bones - venerable and creaky
Exhausted and weary

Eyes bloodshed and teary
Holla if you hear me

Mind

Mind is so blasted
don't know how I've lasted
What a bastard I am
jamming knowledge in the dome
expanding stretching beyond flexibility,
beyond ability
Limberness, tenderness
God bless
Less stress as I caress
my intellect . . . respect the offness
the touch of insanity
beyond vanity

It Didn't Happen

You didn't get leered at
or peered at
It didn't happen to you
Nope, you didn't get harassed or groped
It didn't happen to you
You didn't get roughed up
or bullied
demeaned or sullied
You didn't get followed or accused
or used and abused
It didn't happen to you

Sunken

In a dark place, a sunken area,
where they bury ya
Pain overtaking
my every movement and thought
I've fought

trudging on
through the madness
through sadness
fear and fate

Liver Damage

Pressing on my temples
like menthol hovering over
nasal passages
savages
demons creeping through my cerebrum
won't allow me to be
perky, happy
The weight of these scoundrels
pressing against my eyeballs
contributing to my downfall
Spruce me up with chemical spheres
in an attempt
to control the matter between my ears
I fear
I'll suffer in the future
with sutures
to repair the damage of living -
Liver Damage
I manage to press on
resisting the pressure
nothing can measure
the pain felt after
regretful words dealt
How do I deal with the appeal of finality?
Ending it

Depressing

Confessing
It's depressing
Having you guessing
and stressing
The pain,
depression
agonies in succession

Untitled

Suicidal, my mind idle
Tasty thoughts, scrumptious
memories, indemnities
Serenity, surrealness
feel this, amiss-ness
trouble atop trees
breezy branches, swaying
flights, delaying

Could This Be?

Sometimes I feel as though
I'll end up lonely
I'll be by myself, no one will know me
I struggle to comprehend
why my brain is so complex
I travel from one thought to the next
I want to find out who that man is
I see him every day,
but yet don't know who he is

This man knows of his everyday actions
and knows why he acts
He is my height and complexion
and never looks back
I can see him; he is very content and blessed
He has been victorious in life's contest
He stands alone with independence, but
connected to woman and child
A family, troubles are mild

I believe I get closer to this man everyday
Someday I will find him, I pray
I watch his expressions with envy
He is so complete, joyous and happy

Myself, sometimes I feel manic
but yet relaxed, never in a panic
Just depressed and thoughts of violence

thoughts of death and thoughts of silence
Disappointed of my actions and my nightmares
for me to be in good spirits is somewhat rare

What keeps me going is the vision of that man
and our pleasant meeting
I will finally find out his identity
Could this man possibly be me?

Chapter 5:
Color Blind

"As long as my love is

healthy

    that truly makes me

wealthy"

Wallace Johnson

See Me

Come and talk to me
Come and share a drink
to see how I think
Come and exchange with open mind
Open your heart with my kind
See me for a human that's being
ambitious
not unnerving or vicious
See me as a mentor,
doctor, inventor
View me as a dad . . . the center
Picture me, not framed
Ashamed to draw conclusions
See me in real-time
not a false illusion
Witness the unknown
We're different, no clones
Break through the yellow tape
and forget what you've heard of
The robberies, incarceration and murders
Listen intensely, hear me
Embrace us, don't fear me

Pigment

Let me supply you with some facts,
some facts about being Black
You may act
like you don't know, but you do
We roll with a so-called "crew"
while you go out with your "buddies"
We live where everything be muddy and scummy
You think we dummies?

Are we really all the same?
Oh no-
Your hair is straight
I sport a fro
More pigment, melanin -
different skin
We listen to hip-hop and R & B
You listen to AC/DC
Stereotypes that seem true,
I am different from you
and you are different from me
Do you agree?

Same color blood
but not dermis
Your hair is straight
but I would have to perm this
We occupy the same space
My race, your race, your place, my place

Black face
White face
Red Blood
Red Blood
The heart is the center
Necessity, like the placenta
What's within is what matters,
You've seen my blood splatter

But all must unify in order to advance,
have a better chance
Not conform, but form
Head to college dorms
Buy stock
You stop makin rocks
and no one will sell 'em
Gotta keep down the swellin

We need some sort of treaty or truce
so that we can all sip the juice
I'm tired of bein' the caboose
while you engineering
I hear my people cheering
cause I'm scoring
We are all enduring
Oppression

The Description

You fit the description
      I'm thinking:
        Tall, dark and handsome
You fit the sketch
      I'm thinking:
        Yes, I'm a great catch
Sorry but you fit the profile
        Sure muscular, nice smile

You fit the description
Tall, Black and frightening
Black, Black and Black

Intrigue

Why you eye-ballin me?
What? You like what you see?
Didn't your father teach you
not to look at me?
Are you attracted to my cocoa?
Or are you mesmerized by my vocals?
Do I intrigue you because I am different?
Do you wonder-
if my manhood can bring the thunder?
What attracts you? Why do you stare?
Is it the texture of my hair?
Is it the shape of my nose?
The size of my lips?
Do you wonder if my genes come equipped?
Are you interested in my bouts with society?
Maybe you are into variety
I hope your attraction to me is genuine - real
If you could just feel what I feel,
then there can be true empathy
You could see what I see!
Sadly, I am aware that color exists
It is a shame that it brings fists,
guns too, creates barriers
aggressiveness and anger, like pit bull terriers
You and me, it ain't just experimental
It is mental
We embrace the pigment
We stopped being ignorant

Black Kid

I walk in, got you distracted
you're attracted
Black kid
from the suburbs
No consumption of liquor or herbs
Good career
"His children I'll rear"
Few dates, time flies
gazing eyes
clutching
lips touching
no mistakin this
Nakedness
approval
garment removal
feeling, giving
stealing, living

Color Blind

Darkness, the absence of light
Blindness, the absence of sight
Color blindness, the sight of black and white
This aspect like the depth of night
Her skin, silky, but of unimportance
Her skin, creamy white, but of no relevance
Stereotypical, he can dance
Stereotypical, she has a better chance
His skin, a lighter shade of black,
but of unimportance
His skin, smooth,
but of minute relevance
A strong emotion governs two colors
This same emotion reigns over two lovers
Outside forces seek to intervene,
attempting to discourage the King and the Queen
Something within repels these forces
the power within, yes the heart is the source
The source of power as that of the sun
enough power to convert two into one
Unity of the color spectrum
of utmost importance
Unity of humanity
of extreme relevance
Colorblindness, thought to be a deficit
Ironically, it is one of God's greatest gifts

Through the Eyes Of

Just because I am of the same persuasion
doesn't mean I can't admire you on occasion
Just because I am the same gender
doesn't mean I can't view you with splendor
My pupils widen from sights of your sexuality
Is it a strike against morality?
I know the pieces of the puzzle don't connect,
maybe that's why we get no respect
We aren't recognized in matrimony
They don't know you or me

It is not my choice, it is innate,
my gender increases my heart rate
I always wanted to adhere to the norm
but my heart would not let me conform
I remember when I realized
that the pieces didn't fit
because they were not opposite
This can't be right because civilization would end
if everyone had the same sex friend
But this feels so right and God gave me feelings
I can't control that I find you appealing

Who may judge us
for we are all on the same level?
Who are you to say
my actions are that of the Devil?
So quick to say because I am different,

I am wrong
Discrimination, society's song
Shouldn't love be the focus?
Powerful like the swarm of the locust?
As long as my love is healthy
that truly makes me wealthy
What I see and what you see
send different signals to the brain
I try to fight it, but I can't refrain

I Shave My Face

Am I a man because I can beat someone's ass?
Am I a man because I can pull a gun and blast?
Am I a man because the testosterone is pumpin?
Am I a man because I am running and jumpin?
Or is a man one who takes care of his own?
One who has made mistakes and grown?

What makes a man?

Society distorts this picture
The real man is always the victor
If you don't prevail,
you've got your head in your tail
Better yet, show you're "hard!" - go to jail
Violent heroics by men on screen
leave little boys with lofty dreams
Can I save the leading lady, put evil to rest
and walk away with a medal on my chest?

In the weight room constantly
building shoulders and pecs
Expected to have enduring sex
and risk our necks
bring home hefty paychecks
Yeah, I know, today
there are a lot more female breadwinners
and significantly less that prepare dinner
but still there are great burdens on our minds

wine and dine, save mankind
Mow lawns, munch rugs
We can't hug!
Oh no! That would make us soft
Go to work even though you got a viscous cough

Play hurt! Do more damage! Block out pain!
No way am I comin' out of this game!
Got too much to lose
So what if I can't walk!
I can still talk
Be physical
Be rough
Be tough
Take charge! Be the aggressor!
Block out the constant stressors
Make her earth quake
Firm hand shake
Look them in the eye
Real men don't die
and they definitely don't cry

You Deserve Me

You deserve me
Just serve me
Serve me in the workforce
Serve me in the kitchen
Serve me in the hospitals
With hospitality
like it's your mission
Serve me in society
With equitable morality

We deserve us
at the same table
capable of breaking bread
capable of joining heads
Serve me at the fountains
Serve me at the counters
We deserve peaceful encounters

Didn't You See

Didn't you see?
They didn't ask the person in front of me
for their ID
What was all the buzz?
Why was it so important to know who I was?
Or who I am
Was she not as important as me?
Is that why you didn't require ID
Or where I'm going -
it kills you not knowing
or being in control
of my soul
Nooo . . . It must be me
Can't you see?
Here is my ID . . .
and my dignity

People of No Color

People of no color
Can you be an ally
not sitting idly by?
Will you yell from the hills
when unarmed black men are killed?
Can you show the same disgust
for that which is unjust -
the same loathing you display
when they remove a statue or a bust?

People of no color
Can you advocate
for the marginalized and promote anti-hate?
Will you be just as repulsed
when an officer extinguishes a pulse?
Can you show the same abhorrence
to the oppressed circumstance
as when an object is vandalized -
and you exhibit such despise?

People of no color
Will you attempt to fulfill
what the constitution purportedly promises and
what the founders quilled?
Can you show the same anger you had

as when players knelt before flags?

People of no color
Will you be not hypocritical?
Together we must denounce all hate
It's critical

Colors

I'm inviting things
that are frightening
That which is uncomfortable
I sit at the table
I want to peel it back
and see all the layers
Thwart the naysayers
Blinded
by the colors
so you can't see the others
That's why you're unable
to partake at the table

Chapter 6: Blind

"Use your sharp

thoughts

as a tool"

Wallace Johnson

Big Willy

Who do you think you are?
You tempt me with your fancy cars
You showcase your fancy attire
wanting us to call you sire
You poison the masses with your negative antics
causing the weak to go frantic
pushing poison to your own race
How do you look in my face?
I am a Black child, you are my role model
I see you consume the liquid from bottles
In the ghetto, you are king
Us young boys watch you buy many things
dipped in gold and expensive clothes
Maybe I too can sell that stuff
you put in your nose
You know! That white powder that makes you fly
Sometimes I've even seen some die
Or maybe you can hook me up
with some cannabis sativa
I'll be playin all the sexy divas
You see, to me you are the man
I see you devour prime rib, while I eat out of cans
So what up? Can you put me down?
Maybe I can sell or make drop offs down town?
I want those dead green guys
I want kids to look at me
with the same envious eyes you see.

It becomes a cycle
when we kill each other
Last year I lost my only brother
I know there are no silver spoons in the hood
Brother, just tryin to make good
But it ain't all about monetary figures
"C.R.E.A.M" don't make you bigger
It takes a tougher man to work every day
You're more apt to see your hair turn gray

Clones

Some of these stars are dumb
thinkin they got stardom
Prices skyrocketing
Dudes just mockin men
from old school
Can't mine their own jewels
Boys bandin together sellin out to sell cd's
thinkin they somebody cuz they on TV
Shit what happened to makin your own?
We even got sheep cloned
Can't even coin your own phrase to make coin
Dudes constantly replicating
duplicating
stealin
lyrics got no feeling

Blood Orange

I'd LOVE to eat an orange
and crush it in my teeth
For so long, I've longed to
swallow it beneath
I'd KILL to take this orange
just once and devour
IT into tiny bits
as it sours and cowers
All the wiser,
grinding the pulp
with the friction of my incisors

Sometimes

Sometimes I feel like perishing
for a cause
Just cause the infuriation
causes me such irritation
and it's so frustrating
to lack the domination
to actually affect the situation
It's enraging
I long for alleviation
I want to explode into a frenzy
demolish and destroy the enemy
Sometimes I'm forced to get numb
or I might just succumb
Sometimes I want go postal
and get hostile
but I know it's costly
Will definitely cost me
some time

Jail Bird

Criminals leave minimal
impacts on brats
minute influences on truants
On sabbatical, leaving seeds radical and irrational
Seeds growing in odd directions
because of non-existent affection
Cooped up in cells. Brain cells distorted,
contorted
Broken institutions, retribution, and execution
True sin, abandonment of kin
Offspring sing off tune, negativity consumes
Moon never full, tides never controlled
Drama with no one to play this role
Black cursive ink
explaining how you think
Visits on occasion
don't heal the abrasions
You had to win bread
was your excuse for the abuse
The yeast wouldn't rise. Seeds now despise.
The lies, the bad guys. Non-existent prize.
No male influence or role model
Flashbacks of drugs, full throttle
and empty bottles

Panic

Make no mistake
It's fake
Panic
with no outbreak

C.O.

Is reform really the goal
or is it about control?
We engage them
cage them
enrage them
Is restitution really the purpose of
correctional institutions
or is it to stifle and control populations?
Is it to maintain the pecking order
of our divisive nation?
We imprison minds and souls
for maintenance of control
even on parole
or probation
it all fits the calculation
of the 13th amendment
penned cleverly to keep them servants

Prisoner

Poundin the pavement, clean shaven
quest for a new haven
to exhibit my superior skills
to produce the mils,
meals
What the deal?
No one else feelin me?
They should be stealin me
I'm cheap at the present
They feel resentment
In my prime, focused, willing, eager
  Not qualified
  Nice resumé
but resume
  Carry on
Must be that one question: Felon?
Answer: Yes
My melon hurts. No gamble
So I ramble

Judge

To you -
thugs sport tattoos
Two earrings
means he sings
off tune
Hood pulled up -
up to no good
Corn rows, oh no,
must be headed to death row
Short skirt -
She wants to flirt
Provocateur
had it coming to her

Be the Example

Can you do something not explicit?
Be not complicit
in the detriment
to the youngins?
So tongue 'n cheek
They say the meek
not the weak
shall rule
Use your sharp thoughts as a tool
Don't contribute to the tomfoolery
All about jewelry
and money
Appreciate the sunny
days and sets
and the ocean's wetness
Waves crashing
smashing
barriers, ceilings
wielding
guns and knives
negatively affecting lives

Chapter 7: Insight

"**If you claim**

to follow Jesus

inclusivity

is what He preaches"

A
jus
Lo
mer
Walk
Seek
Fight the
Defend the
Love
neigh
as I lo
Save th
Be stror
courage
not be
because

Look, I am

t
ly
ve
cy
humbly
justice
oppressor
fatherless
thy
bor
ve you
needy
g and
ous. Do
terrified
of them

coming soon!

Satanic Verses

Satan rules the Earth in its last days
To the almighty Lord, you best give praise

Satan rules the Earth with selfish sinners
You best say grace at suppers and dinners

Satan rules the Earth
through two thousand and ten
God help all women and men

Satan rules the Earth with liars and cheaters
God help those batterers and beaters

Satan rules the Earth with promiscuity and greed
To all rules of morality, you must take heed

Satan rules the Earth
with spontaneity and confusion
To allow outsiders in the temple
is a tragic intrusion

Satan rules the Earth with the slightest energy
We must all come together and create synergy

Bi-Partisan Bird

Left wing, Right wing -
we're one fowl being
in the middle,
flying in the same direction
despite the opportune view,
clouded by visible differences
soaring but soured by invisible variables
The peak of the pecking order
fowl with disorder
Left wing, Right wing
The other side of the aisle
Gliding, coasting
Boasting, roasting
All the while
attached in the middle

Picking

The birds will pick at me
flesh in their beaks
God speaks
to me
I seek solace in our meeting
the fowl smell, the eating
picking, needling at my crevices
seeking value with ever-sharp caresses
tugging and pulling me away
from the bones
As I seek flight in the clouds
shrouds of guilt overcast me
thoughts of penance outlast me

Heaven

When I leave this Earth
I want to be floatin, not fallin
I wanna hear the good Lord callin
I'll be on the judgment list
Hell took many shots at me, but missed
Heaven aimed and fired
and got who they desired

I hope to be God's priority
along with the minority
Please let my family follow
or eternal life will be sadly hollow

Can't wait to see the face
responsible for my being
This will be a sight truly worth seeing

Hope I'm not rejected
Bright lights like expected?
Will that entity see me with a gleam in eye?
Did the rules I abide by?
The world is in its last days
Did I live in God-like ways?
Will I be waved on or greeted with a handshake?
As long as I don't fall into that fiery lake
A lot I did learn
Hope I don't burn
Wanna have the Lord's clearance

when it's my turn

I can see it now, there is a majestic escalator
On the top is the lover, on the bottom - the hater
Once at the top, the Lord decides
if you may pass through
If denied, the bottom falls from beneath you
The rejected will let out horrific screams
while the accepted will fulfill their dreams

6 Foot and Some Inches

Standing over my vehicle with weeping eyes
Paying respects. Why do you cry?
For I've gone to a much better place
No more frowns on this face
Don't wanna witness such pain
Wish my casket were closed
Just moments ago, Viva placed a rose
on the center of my cold, lifeless chest
She's coming to grips
that soon I will be laid to rest
and Mort stop getting all misty
I know damn well you won't miss me
In the past I've kinda felt imprisoned
but now my soul has risen
They gather around me thinking I have died
but I'm only traveling to the other side
I'm returning to that which created me
6 feet down, the earth will swallow me

Grounded

When they put me in the ground
my heart will no longer pound
Not another sound
No more beating
No more mistreatment
No longer harassed,
shocked or gassed
Surpassed for promotion
not elected or hired
unjustly fired
No more being tired
of scratching and clawing
gnashing and gnawing
When they place me in the earth
reverse of my birth
the curse will disperse
My soul immersed
with glorious treasures
that can't be measured
When they place me in the earth
I will know my worth
When I'm lowered into the ground
Silence, not another sound

He Sees You

If you claim
to follow Jesus
inclusivity
is what he preaches
His love forever reaches
You may not judge or exclude
or eliteness exude
Requirements are
be humble and forgiving
to all that are living
No matter your features
Love all God's creatures

See Through

You put on your Sunday best
on a quest
to see Jesus
Oh Jesus! is laughing at thee
with all your blasphemy
Your dressed down best
I guess
isn't good enough so you believe
sinfully suited in your sharp seersucker
you have to be a sucker to believe
that your parents are non-transparent
and apparently you can cover up
ugly with cover girl and majestic hats
high heels and flats
He sees you
He sees right through

Your Demise

One day they gonna tell the story of your
demise
through crying eyes
video montages
flowers, not corsages
What legacy are you leaving?
Achievements
soften the bereavement

Off of me

Clashing bodies
as they cashed in
Warriors sweating and bleeding
needing to provide
Feeding the strikes to the bellies
Devastating as the smashing of minds
Lifting the bodies
off the bloody canvases
painted by the con-artists of mankind
Grappling with the decisions
blinding blows, blurring the visions
Making a mockery of me
as I misplace my memory
I'm getting closer to the prophet
as you profit
and get . . . off of me

While I'm Here

While I'm here,
let's live without fear,
attention to what is dear
Hear my voice
by choice -
not burden

**Counteract Division
with clear Vision**

**Choose Unity
to strengthen Community**